Walloping Shrug

Also by Scott Keeney

Early Returns

Pickpocket Poetica

Sappho Does Hay(na)ku

Walloping Shrug

POEMS 1994–2000

Scott Keeney

SOME CLOUDS PRESS

Copyright © 2018 Scott Keeney

Part II of this book was previously published as a pdf chapbook (2004) and an online blogbook (2007) under the title *The Once Invisible Conclusion*.

Book design by Scott Keeney
Typeset in Weiss Std

ISBN 978-1-948728-91-1 (paperback)
ISBN 978-1-948728-90-4 (ebook)

for KC

CONTENTS

Acknowledgments · xi

Prologues

Poeta Nascitur Sed Fit · 3

That We Ain't Ever Been · 4

Tag · 5

I

Meditation on the Death of Hart Crane · 9

Note to Self · 10

The Magician · 11

The Whale Watcher · 12

One Form of Love, Perhaps · 13

Homage to William Stafford · 14

Something from Nothing · 15

Main St. · 16

Heatwave · 17

The Legend of Treat · 18

A Song of the Sun · 19

Night Song · 20

Five Haiku Centos · 21

Five More Haiku Centos · 22

What's Left · 23

The Philosopher · 24

Postcard to Chris Mulia · 25

The New Bohemians · 26

II

The Once Invisible Conclusion · 29

Light Dies in the Eyes · 30

Dawn Overflows Some Distance from Here · 31

One Infinity at a Time · 32

Like Smoke I Drag · 34

A Long Way from All Comes One · 35

Erect Tongue / Muffled Church · 37

My Will Sharpened and Blunted · 38

Lullaby Sentence · 39

Translated into a Finger on the Lips · 40

Phoenix / Records · 41

Have Hands Will Rust I Must Confess · 42

To the Fierce Laughter of the Mountains · 43

Chorus of Wild / Flowers behind Eyes · 44

Blue Sun / Set the Boundaries Never Mind · 45

III

A Sizable Wallop · 49

IV

Route · 61

Mystery and Melancholy of a Street · 62

The Secret of Flight, a Triptych · 64

Vault · 65

Access · 66

Pop Music Epistemology and the Prospect of Virtual Being · 67

Subterranean Apartment Blues · 69

An Origin · 70

All Right, Then, I'll Go To Hell · 71

Some Resemblance Acquired · 73

Epithalamium · 74

Outstretched Streetlight Aqua Serenade · 75

The Lover · 76

Against the Years of Great Momentum and Loss · 77

Nirvana Rondeau Cento · 78

What Whole? What Sum? What Parts? · 79

Peaceward Recoil · 80

Poem · 81

Late · 82

Part · 83

ACKNOWLEDGMENTS

My thanks to the editors of the publications in which the following poems previously appeared, sometimes in different versions or under different titles:

Carriage House Review: The New Bohemians

Conatus: Homage to William Stafford; Meditation on the Death of Hart Crane

Dirigible: Chorus of Wild / Flowers behind Eyes; Blue Sun / Set the Boundaries Never Mind

Elm: The Magician

The End Review: Epithalamium; Some Resemblance Acquired

E·ratio: What Whole? What Sum? What Parts?

Eye-Rhyme: Late

Gestalten: Erect Tongue / Muffled Church; The Secret of Flight, a Triptych

Helix: One Form of Love, Perhaps

Lost and Found Times: Against the Years of Great Momentum and Loss

Mid-America Poetry Review: Poem

Milk: Route; Vault

New York Quarterly: Poeta Nascitur Sed Fit

Poetry East: Subterranean Apartment Blues

Rio: Phoenix / Records

Shampoo: Part

Shattered Wig Review: Translated into a Finger on the Lips

The Silver Web: Heatwave; The Legend of Treat; Main St.

Skanky Possum: All Right, Then, I'll Go To Hell; Outstretched Streetlight Aqua Serenade

Tight: Dawn Overflows Some Distance from Here; The Once Invisible Conclusion; Light Dies in the Eyes

21 Stars Review: Nirvana Rondeau Cento

Ugly Duckling: One Infinity at a Time; A Long Way from All Comes One

We: Tag

Zaum: Pop Music Epistemology and the Prospect of Virtual Being

And to imagine a language is to imagine a form of life.
Ludwig Wittgenstein

Walloping Shrug

PROLOGUES

POETA NASCITUR SED FIT

for Chris Mulia

Stark minded and spiritually naked, Allen Ginsberg
once said in an interview in I forget where but
I remember reading it on the floor in the library
at the Waterbury branch of UConn when I was
nineteen and didn't yet know that "Howl" exists,
a poem is the greatest gift a person could give
to another person or any animal for that matter
I'm sure he would have sung that last part in there
had it been relevant or at least on his mind at the time,
it doesn't matter that Ginsberg was young and
living in the city on bread and water and wine,
Benzedrine and tea, that doesn't discount the fact
that poems exist to be shared and stored away
or stored away and shared at a later date under
naked stars, and if there are no stars out over the next
young poet's apartment there are always rats
naked in the stairwell or behind stark walls,
the poet scared at first to death, naked and drunk
on wine or dreams of drinking wine and rolling
down hillsides with Li Po or howling at guards
from the rooftops, killing time with Rimbaud,
as the words tumble through his feminine lips
like slippery pigs in all of their oh well splendor,
Stark mad and raving naked, I thought I was a girl . . .

THAT WE AIN'T EVER BEEN

I was eatn lions
I was suckin grass
All my minds were up my ass
Like a train
This locomotive ka-boom
I was turtle shell happy
Singin Jazz to the rain
When a light came from behind me
To illuminate these keys
On which I type
Like the iron of night
My fall is Dear, dear
All I want is for you
To be aware
I am the zany gone cat
Lickin at your slippers
For a bite to eat
If you don't mind
Mind
I am the type
To speed up at any moment
And drop like a plum
The sorrow of the world
A bicycle chain
Trying to catch up
With itself
I am after you
Like a bad, bad dream
It's sad
That we ain't ever been

TAG

Over now under
the T the streets
like Renaissance artists
stretch seaward

Sky pulled tight
as the skirt
of the Ally McBeal
standing hmm
across the aisle

Riding a train's
a subtle dance

HELLO my name is
The Cities
by Paul Blackburn

I

MEDITATION ON THE DEATH OF HART CRANE

      The dove with tired, drunken eyes,
Beyond blown pain and far between two lands,
Hey non nonny and by ecstasy gone,
Watching the ocean, its sick flowers, churn.

The white petals having spun themselves
Open, soft and vital Atlantis reveal;
A glance of desert under palm-wheel shade,
The inviting eye of steep tomorrow's end.

Ever with dawn imprinted on his wings
Which both sun and sea have chanced approach,
He's now too low, too sodden to fly—only
An effortless drop under the abraded sky.

NOTE TO SELF

No, heartbreaker, don't be alarmed.
The door has swung open, but
nothing has entered and nothing
was behind it, not even a breeze.

The window is not reflecting
the shadow of your assassin
or a reverse angle of the sun
or the red eyes of your father.

In fifteen minutes the clock
will not strike a significant hour,
the dog will not begin to bark,
and the birds will still avoid you.

Let your only concern be whether
the walls will translate from
the summer leaves all that you need
to know to survive the winter.

THE MAGICIAN

Chilled champagne trickles down
your spine, and for a moment
you fear for the rabbit
yanked suddenly into this world.

How many doves can possibly fly
out of the magician's impossible
sleeve? And how can such vital flowers
spring from that same secret nest?

How many scarves can he twist
into flames of contradiction? How
many rings can his fanatic hands
unbind? And how, always,

can he pluck the ace of solace
from behind your ear?—Even now
while his fingertips alight
on the hairs of the back of your neck

like little steam engines
that drive you into his top hat
where you come across nothing
in its symphonic black balm.

THE WHALE WATCHER

That was no belly rising from black eternity,
no smoked Buddha spreading light across the sea,
though rays entangled threads of yellow, red, and green
around the imperfect, dimpled fold of spleen
that cracked the slate of the water encumbered by
the whisper of dawn between horizon and machine.

The sun on my face and on the slick coats of us all,
we tightly-wrapped tourists keeping ourselves warm
from the spurts of spitting wind; a child, the only one
who saw that humpback caught in the sun's reflections,
the alchemy of water and light into gold, I saw
the hard curve, the tear, ripping the ocean.

ONE FORM OF LOVE, PERHAPS

We were parked near the docks,
some spot she knew in West Haven,
looking out at the surgent waves
with The Doors on the radio
singing "Let's swim to the moon"
between clouds, eye-level bright
and inviting us not out but into
each other, hands and mouth,
and it's so hard to believe now
how it all really happened so
perfect like that, except for when
she unsnapped my pants and took
out my cock and stroked it
long and hard with her rings still on.
Later, when I used the bathroom
across from her room, I checked
and saw I was cut in a couple
of places, and I wondered if
maybe I should have said something.

HOMAGE TO WILLIAM STAFFORD

When the words come to you,
Write them down. When the walls
Crumble, let them fall.
His voice tells me in a dream.

As when the sunless sky
Tints the white libraries red,
The words should procession
Through your head, already cleared;

As when, stepping out
Into the pre-dusk blue,
You regard the ring-billed gulls
Cursing through the air,

Let the walls crumble
In back of you
Before the spectacle of flight—
The white scavengers drifting

Beyond sight, into the void
Where something remains of words.

SOMETHING FROM NOTHING

I can imagine the other side
of any tree or any moon
the horizon wraps around me
like daylight savings time.

The rain rises to the earth
and sounds like buttons,
the unbuttoning of a sweater—
love's muscle memory.

The west wind is out of season
but I am due for a poem
and here I am in the middle
of this park getting wet.

The leaves themselves sound
something like goodbye
as if they were written by Verlaine
to be read at such a time.

Indeed, it's dark o'clock
far beyond any earth
I can imagine the other side
of almost any given door.

MAIN ST.

A turtle
walking
a bearded
angel

might look
like a clock
striking
twelve

but really
it's just
the metronome
to which

our lives
are burning
insects in
a microwave

HEATWAVE

A staircase leading nowhere,
going on forever. I turn
to hear the cicadas seething
like lightbulbs going out.

Over every mantle there's
a mirror and in every mirror
there's a clock. And in
every second that's lost

nothing happens. I think
I'm ecstatic when I'm nude.
I thank your gods when you
are, my love. In this heat,

I open up like an envelope
stuffed with popular ideas—
I am the pendulum more
than time is. I am the ice

cream melting in the sun;
eyes, dogs in hazy always.
My love, why are you out
shopping in this weather?

THE LEGEND OF TREAT

What am I to make of this La-la Land?
Crickets seethe like lightbulbs.
Stapled to the sky with a sparkling,
what might be called my soul.
I have to laugh at the fountain tonight,
toast a *Bufo americanus*—no, tomorrow.
Mind and object are both
"buried in the fragrant hash of imitation."
A precipice's falling. My neither eye!
I long to pacific shiny the pain
to see how everything cackles in light,
"such a textbook." It's all so insignia,

so overflowingly meridian: this kingdom,
though one trudges through its junkyards,
pimples with the inspiration of poor health.
The sky is more than everything to me.
The hums of distant cars gently hammer
away at my brain like an unmentioned rose.
When the wind blows I stick out my tongue
and make silly faces. Is that a penny
rattling around in the left ventricle of my heart?
Soon I will imitate a sparrow, then a troll.

A SONG OF THE SUN

after Gregory Corso

The sun is the morningest
song in the morning
when the earth is as tired
as the earth of these eyes.

Lucky as a man who has
found another man
or woman who loves and
brings out the woman in him,

the sun that's the same sun
mooning us with moonlight
shall rise above tomorrow
until tomorrow goes splat.

NIGHT SONG

after Ma Lihua

Sun gone down, and the mountains
the creatures of the zodiac
creep over, into the indigo sea.

I am those stars, scattered, only
to disappear at daybreak,
chasing now, or chillin' on the shore.

Loneliness. I've said it. The night
makes you beautiful like a street
cloaked with revelers.

The small clouds like whole notes
through the dark, almost
like leaves, almost

like me, if I were shivering
like I should be
by now.

FIVE HAIKU CENTOS

Sweat-bead upon your belly
by the light of a fifteen-watt bulb.
You were going to ask me something.

    * * *

A rumbling motor.
Sparrows look up and fly off.
I will be nice to you.

    * * *

Dirty black dungarees
in the blue light of the television screen.
I'm thinking of you, your eyes.

    * * *

Bent, bent grass
beyond the reach of the sun's rays.
I hear a tired voice.

    * * *

Just enough light to make out
through the rain and mud
your absence.

FIVE MORE HAIKU CENTOS

A hawk on a boulder
Your face in the lake
Under my hair is a brain

      *   *   *

A small bird hops about in branches
around a corner, exhaust clouds billowing
again and again, I kiss her orange ear

      *   *   *

Low clouds cut off the sun
In the shadow of your breath
I know what's slipping through my fingers

      *   *   *

The filthy piles of snow are melting
Ah, the desert in bloom
You were here yesterday

      *   *   *

A small wind
through dirty windows
I want what is left

WHAT'S LEFT

Perfect moon in the sky
And petals falling . . .
I am on the bus!

    *   *   *

clouds go rolling over
smells nice
but I don't give a fuck

    *   *   *

All the leaves are black
As the sun passes behind the mountains
I drink a glass of wine

    *   *   *

cigarettes and money
a bird comes to the window
the chime goes unheard

    *   *   *

The light is dim
beneath the big red cedar
Machines rise and descend

THE PHILOSOPHER

Dark rainy, how much do I miss the sun
with its carnival antics and relative heat?
My allergies are acting out today.
I have this need, or is it desire,
to start all over, erase the first line
and set down a new one that works.
Gray drain, thoughts of lines dot
disappear. Turn the water on and
the pipes will knock. I mean,
you have to expect certain things
like regrets and changing your clothes.
I know that, but my heart
won't hear what my brain is saying.

POSTCARD TO CHRIS MULIA

You'll notice the many clouds in the sky.
I like to think of them as flowers. I'm sure
you understand. You might have to squint.
We call the play of light on the surface
of the water in our toilet The Hand
of God in a Nutshell. By the way,
we miss you and hope you'll join us soon.
I'm putting together a book of poems
(by other poets) just for you.
Remember to think of them as something
other than flowers, perhaps fish
struggling on a hook, no throwing back.
Even up here the wildest dreams have
nothing to do but read books on the toilet.
I know what you're thinking, but this
ain't no movie we're starring in! So
let's all get together, go to the city and
laugh art sometime. See 7th line, Scott.

THE NEW BOHEMIANS

They cultivate madness à la Rimbaud
So that they might capture in words
The ballet of body parts
Thrashing through the mosh pit.

Otherwise they hang out on headstones,
Throwing their empties
Through the fog
At their own graffiti on the walls.

Eightballs buried
Behind their eyes—
When the moon winks
They look agog—

They want
To paint the night
As if death were an art gallery
With no art.

II

THE ONCE INVISIBLE CONCLUSION

when even the dawn's fingers are blue
fruits without stems
the rubber seeds of revelation
near a glass of water on the kitchen counter
breathing like a plastic bag in the wind
my obelisk has reached into
the blue horizon's ripping clouds again
however gnarled the grass may be
the opium of creation
and every year waiting for correspondence
when I feel gory heaven I feel as if
awakened under chain or fork
can only grunt as Rocky Balboa would
the swampy streets send up
cigarette butts misunderstandings dark glass
whatever constitutes my soul today
through walls of collapsing
the fruit blue on the window sill
carry the mirror with both hands
through a cave like the future
a lichen of blood on my shadow
dice rattling overhead
I pace to exterminate nostalgia's gray carpet
eyes barbecued to a temple
gathered only a prehistoric amusement
grace found in bridges of laughable news
a blue spot growing on my belly

LIGHT DIES IN THE EYES

gypsy tune of the evening's eyelashes
over the lush creeping hills
a black strand of hair on a paper plate
algebraic shadows of solemn trees
bedspring breaths in the trenches
of both fountains of the present
I throw my crayons at the moon
the sky as affectionate as any canvas
a suicide window opens into
the way an empty suitcase looks
and all the rivers desire young lovers
for a chorus to fool around with
a garden of half-erased words
the dogs on the horizon come good-byes
as lightning laughs all down my arm
I am the undercurrent and compass
of the tune blue in the face of absence

DAWN OVERFLOWS SOME DISTANCE FROM HERE

a dog's bark from the bow of day
the wine has left a bloody variable on my t-shirt
I keep a pebble tucked in my change pocket
maybe dead plums are my passion
and what is in me burns like a billion years
library of automatic pain
stairs under orris and anesthesia
the sand is green the moon
umbrellas and various other angels
on winds that deny the female sky
eyes throat and nose on fire it's lithium season
I snarve and the horizon smiles
always bound and crowded the body's child
a pair of upright eggs mind and object jump
together in the house where the noise is always real
there's no mirror like a dirty pebble
the pathos of bongos because it is yesterday
already my angel is asking me to
but I can't even landscape the epiphany
from windows and dreams breath lingers longest
I'd like to locate each small wing
lose it from above or below and begin my special effects
pressing the right keys and turning
myself into writing a poem at the moment I die
to be bewildered Siddhartha Gautama

ONE INFINITY AT A TIME

no shadow falls the sun is parsley
in passing there is one tough
I always feel for all the marbles
snatch up the lamentations
clams in my eyes so candles oozed
faded into the banks of the sky
the footsteps smell like gutters
are no longer forgotten
a bonfire running across the floor with away
converging into shame
is etched in the candelabra of my mind
large spattered extenuations
along with sunflowers and my need
filled with money some squashed worms
my dreams might be purified
I believe a butterfly
above anxious paperdews
in the university squares in early ideas
such winds are to be expected
another moment before death
no wider than a salt shaker
and I must both come and go
clouds lap the horizon
blue landscapes are my cells today
the women inside me paint my penitentiary
cellophane for the sad moon
and random fruits
like arms flailing in the distance

the boats will be all
into the grain of each overwhelming
with no living grass
the holes of words instead of worms
and birds that rejoice in eating the stars

LIKE SMOKE I DRAG

the use of birds is not metaphorical
cobwebs and a doorknob
out there the wind hurts the leaves to the ground
I see words in the night after tomorrow
two tomatoes and a cabbage
pale smoke lofting over the clergyman of my youth
I'm not even half a century old
who says the window's clean and the cast is
in ecstasy if I could swallow
my testicles and a reflection from a medusan garden
I trade my free will in elevators
which is why I live for the week ends
scarecrow in the apple tree
a red and white table cloth stretched into constellations
the birds come back and I can tell
they are sparrows or cardinals or maple leaves or crows
about the shoe repairs of the world
as it grows in the backrooms of my intuition
the music almost unnoticeably fading out
like a row of streetlights at dawn
the ceramic spanish-dancer in a flourish
just walking down I pass through
orgasms like a glowworm in the shadows of the freeway

A LONG WAY FROM ALL COMES ONE

chance is the mother of the poets
the grass is a solifidian dance
fish are movie cameras behind black
windows of supine elegance
my heart is beating from inside the glass
of water blue in smoke-filtered sunlight
I am not furloughed not thinking like
stems or bones there is a stalk of celery
that is all I have of heavenly sound
to measure the limbs of my hand
I can only guess which shelter
makes me tired after and after some
times I can feel the wrinkled bark
of the dogs meaning on the horizon
tomorrow has been purplish all the day
to know that petals fall like lucifer
disappear into the innocent approached
abstract as the hooker in outer space
and some door opening for me
I enter as a bridge from the silent
every utensil on every table
longing for iridescence because redolence
like an often scarred buttocks
is philosophical and dazed at length
or a photo I want only one face
the forgotten face that can never
ever be seen even if the sky is laminated
with come or grass or gills
any memory of lean tender meat
sound of a leaf scratching the sternum

to want all the world's mail
in a backpack in a matchbox car
the black trees sending up their filaments
jack is not looking to score
only to sell his cash for some seeds The Situation of Gnats as Sparks
    of Something
hives and the pavement and under summer porches
to lie down on the sidewalk and feign death
mosquitoes
the nuances of any given cuticle
to pray the dead will not die that I am breathing in
my ancestors in the kitchen still
singing in the dog's mouth a tennis ball
the carnation in the garbage
I don't know what to do with my hands
in the shower of waiting the forests of northern
africa
the body drinks the water of the city
left on the night stand next to the false teeth
for joy I moan and walk away
who must receive my order by december first
to ensure delivery
draw me a circle please and leave some heart within it
chronologically
a sponge drying on the window sill
I open to an empty room
dream of lipstick on the sky and crawl into bed
at dawn I am the one who is finished
and there is a nervousness about
I at least have this poem

ERECT TONGUE / MUFFLED CHURCH

the way a locust latches itself to vegetation
for what the shells of the day are traded
I once tattooed a stone with my penis
to juggle the words until azure puckers up
the wind is swift as a sunlit lover's lasting kiss
a penny loafer of syncopated Platonism
the dew is yellow with breath I feel
a wheel in the flesh burning through
around the earth in a hand the umbilicus
silver ashes stirring in primavera caves
red as purgatory as a caustic light
the living room of intelligence is rubber
another frigid morning in the eggshell
of this chilling b-movie my awkward
gulls in the moonlit limousine of history
even now I am scuffing this continuum
of embracing the dead in the living
I get caught up in the sorrow of centipedes
contemplation cancels the unnameable
between grins when talismans stay chance
I might be a mystic every time I breathe
the angel is a marble of sustenance
always too the silence of predators
I go where only the dirt passes for blue
the metabolism of fire like the embrace
of a frying pan colors while it fights
against the painful appreciation of smoke
like a mirror might breaking up slowly
the face of heaven the face of hell

MY WILL SHARPENED AND BLUNTED

my will to break the heart of the world with a shrug
my sight is a sock with holes in it
among all those violent heckles and boos
worms are the stars inside
water is boiling on the stove under the six
the surface reflex and corners
begin what is the jaded bird in the sacred bulb
suffering the human pastiche the gone
mystique already I can smell the moss growing
circles please come carve with me
in time become plural
as if the gendered body hides nearer to god's in the hinges
down batterson drive I grow up
with my whimpers' eyes in the shadows crust
again my psyche's lost without
on a bench with the surgeon general's warnings wrapped
the delicate strife that ticktocks my spine
starred with benevolent gingivitis
as such a song is made of
the sun beyond the dream of sunlight or
there is no need like the future
I am ready to fall up out of myself as if all I wanted to return
the wind removes the raindrop west
follow the muskrat of that body's sky blue skin in the paint
of my very own invisible rooms
always from a mousehole
between my teeth I hold the pencap but no pen

LULLABY SENTENCE

the dew from the silk all gendered the wine spilling from
the cork to shoulders rain or shine
as a bluejay skittles before the pines sleeping
baby on a bearskin rug
my eyes offer the body a planet to hold onto
words can't only make me the air
traversing feather I fondle
myself to know the price in dollars and sense of
les fleurs du mal shows a little flame
my eyes fit for a frame of glass
more or less fluff the heart longs for a photograph
and the rings there dark and light
the lights there rigged to enlist the object of the past
an eye a throat a square root
dna
licked open and three blue cats curl out
in the journal of silence and immaculate conceptions
is a child in an empty bottle
clouds make hand-puppet angels wherever that one body goes
the many my god oh what
my eyes see *this* through the arrow of my tongue
silence honest as stone
and the lost jokes of the neanderthals
I recall everything in terms of my experience with magnets
bone after bone hits dirt too soon
a few barbules slashed
enough
already the gum in the head being as volatile nailing
my nerves to a song to a dilapidated wall

TRANSLATED INTO A FINGER ON THE LIPS

I break down all seven doors in the house
of what I believe I pose as a lake
grab the day by its eggs the bad angels
that any common sewer rat could snatch
a gas pump or garbage can nippled orange
windows are sawdust is goodbye now
bone-whipping hairs in the nostrils
up in a sitcom perceives meridian bared
the laughing saint in the limousine
go with Vietnam to the dialectical ball
pencils ashes blue glasses of water
and a wind blows me out of my branches
edges of tapedecks edges of adolescence
and what is in me bellies like a drunk
a monk a lover a rock a pocketful of sand
when that old pawn shop opens up
in midstroke where I resemble a handkerchief
stuffed deep into the bottom drawer

PHOENIX / RECORDS

the immortal bird is vague yet feverish as decades
and to the dervish of leaves
there is a mirror blackened white
eye by eye by eye as if I were rubble
what stony rattle of fear
on the flowers of quiet tongues
for the rain on asian mountains
I am my own flaxen ruins
then in a lurching shadow seems
there is no shall in the nodding of leaves
I come to in the hedges of night
if only I could make my water weather
how the shuddering bones of the haunted
angels to toilets a reflection of love
mudbanks the earth's alligator rags I am
for a stoop of deciduous laughter
to the darkest goldenrod in the world
the lightning and ash bird of my language leaves
to scratch a shadow its silence
appears from shore to shore the way
there is an ocean in every bit of flesh
only a few confetti caves
making every channel shriek in purple
dust in the whispers of room
that's for me a mud and feather home
leaves wings trunk and jewel of fire
smoke cannot explain my records are metaphors
beyond mirror and mantelpiece
and the correspondence of stones or twigs
to the dark air in every lit ear
or the dead bird in every living

HAVE HANDS WILL RUST I MUST CONFESS

the rust will shine through any war and through
these echoes growing in my cupped hands
the lovers in my guts light up cigarettes of meaning
among velvet paintings and yellow dust
nights deathly light as honey smooth the nerves like wasps
their speckled asses facing front
plus the purple breath of the sleeping times the dead
erasers over the caress of every surface
a bit of red-raw feeling removed
which leaves or leaves perfectly nothing behind
the body always wanting but to replace periods with dashes
far along the perishing of pages
the sun and oblivion becomes a trifle
burnt out the days fog
poems on the self-same streets of another century
indeed the close-fisted blows of the moon
pound and resound through the gentle slop
of the atmosphere of our words of our circulatory system
my cuticles grow toward you and only you
it's implied (see figure 1.1)
such flowers claw toward lightness

TO THE FIERCE LAUGHTER OF THE MOUNTAINS

the wind crawls through me through the slopes
only my water is blue with sky light
the shell howls carefully where the brain
flip for the fifty-fifty night the offertory shield
but the wind crawls through the bedrock to sing
we are all obscurity's fires trembling
sleep is almost reluctant to return
almost nobody ever splits it open
is a honeycomb cell of silence in the west
far beyond the sparkling atoms
the philosophical web of December trees
light is conducting two hush wants
with the venomous pretend motions through me
a toddler of wind crawls through the skyscraper
two buttonholes waiting like dry sponges
concentric fields swelling dusty chords
of this chasm I am wandering are awakened
the foghorn rooted in waves like tomorrow
the madness blossoms mouth a swamp

CHORUS OF WILD / FLOWERS BEHIND EYES

to suck the burning sand of hope
the body sucks like sadness
through exhaust determination empties me
of the bright delicate lumber
out and in as if I had to forfeit just
and love without the cartouche of autumn leaves
the balcony mind conjures its poets slowly
and I gibbering through the pipes
of a melted crow a hundred sudden
questionmarks of scattered ashes
thirst warms up overhead white-haired
I get stood up by the hyacinth night-journey
am a fjord in beauty's nation
the plants of ravages of childhood
to run screaming to their inflammation
the drops just can't break through
how doves fucked me in the dark
and under the earth I overheat waiting
like an immortal clock for numbers
to discover the pieces buried in cows
in the night these flowers it's ink
gouty white gunshots of the conflagration
every hum hurts like granite
every cuticle falls to the final home of hot rain
every look begins in a shell
ends slicking over the open wounds of hope

BLUE SUN / SET THE BOUNDARIES NEVER MIND

disappears I could
swooping across the percussion
books of clouds open
a constellation of nails all
in closed thermometer sky
I color in the walls
sun shifts my greens
sparrows fly out of the stone mouths
of wallowing in the music of America
become animal blisters on my hands
from the first moment I heard the bell
of this narrative on television seeing
I am weathered by a primitive song
called wind the length of the dragon's jaw
the translucent limestone maze writhing
as I string handkerchiefs through
my flame is bow-legged and rootless
drunk in a winter skull
where the elements are stapling
the window is still shattering
and it has broken another branch
and the perpetual back of hello and goodbye

III

A SIZABLE WALLOP

Déjà vu. The café crowd digs counterintuitive frowns
Until nob by nob it negotiates thirst for common sense,
So the skinhead standing on the couch in the corner
Thinks he's the next Andy Warhol with all of the Sturm und Drang
Of Andy Kaufman. Behind the cardboard mountains
We have ghosts who seem not to coo or howl
But sing, "Making your way in the world today takes
Everything you've got." Birchbark and breadcrumbs,
Hipbones that feel like lemon–poppy-seed cake,
A lifestyle more suited for a lovebird who travels through
Branching time, clasping the stems of willpower's reward,
One less concerned that the uncommon notion should be a
   destination
In itself meaningful as the everyday vocabulary
Of commerce, but more, and more strategic.

If I resurface in Beverly Hills, I will try not to hit my head on
The manhole, or hate myself. O vagrant bubbles of rain,
What do I mean? How much has the cost of slaves gone
Up? Don't be noncommittal. Hang on to, hold
On to, latch on to the paycheck you're earning if
You have to—but don't. You don't need bread, you don't
Need boots: you need Collapse. The cellophane
Rings, "I'm right in the middle a battle, can't this
Kuwait?" he begs to know. "Blackjack." She sleeps
With a phenomenon without relation to its environment
Or any environment for that matter, for example
A forearm to the Adam's apple and the next thing
We know we're scrambled eggs on the floor beside the Times
New Roman rules and regulations for Lundy's Lane

Bed-and-Breakfast, me and the baby-sitter
Wearing only her bandanna, head like a birdcage . . .

Lovers understand the simple OK of the serial
Comma, the off-season facetiae of the depressurized poet.
Petechiae multiplying, until the pantheon of night
Stands over the felos de se of the fimbrial streets
Of suburban downtowns. We zoom in on the confidante
Smashing her way through her own private *Romeo and Juliet*,
Through the glass door of P.O. Drugstore, opening
Her wrist without noticing ever to what extent
She is, as all the passionate are, planted
In the flowerpot of her lover's face. The wind
Brings goosebumps, chow for now—her face, all openmouthed-
Closemouthed, under openmouthed eggshell eyes.

I gave my love a jonquil because I didn't know what else
To say, "Here, I brought you this jonquil,"
Was all I could jolt out of the jaboticaba tea gyttja
Of thought. Think of Manderley, Tara, Brideshead
Before you decide this is wrong! Break out the honey
And sugar packets of pain, I have a seashell I want to show
You. I call it *Bedsprings like Parakeets*. Put it to your ear and
Know why, and know also that we should sleep together
Right here in the daylight under the periwinkle sky
With the temperature rising to dust and stones°
Amid the purple rockets of heather and decumbent
Stems, nostrils wide with the wet toffy smell
Of pondscum, I promise to appeal to the natural jodhpur—
Joyed pear—of your body, to attend to every lunula
And smooth lumpy contour of your lunatic fringe.

And yet, key moments in the scripture return to us
To remind us of crackdowns on social tolerance,
The way they look different depending on our position
Relative to the ruling class. Hey yeomen
And mice in coolie hats, let's put down our Kalashnikovs
And put on Rachmaninoff, or at least some Hendrix or Nirvana.
Sure, it's difficult to know sometimes, whether to fire back
In astonishment, out of need. Take that silhouetted man
In a trenchcoat, briefcase in hand, loafers splashing down the street
Improbably chased by the words "I am" behind him, is he
For us or against us? The word "data" (followed by a period)
Waiting around the corner—is it there to get him
Or to greet him and welcome him into the film we've been
    watching

For years? We're not prone to chatter inspiring memoir
Anymore than a petal-shaped breeze skimming
Along the Mad River as it cuts through the Brass City
Turning their motto, *Brass endures*, into a punchline—
What errancy! He always assumed he sat like a keyboard
On the banks of the river, never to be seen,
Where he fled as a hooligan on the run from the repercussions
Of such adolescent shenanigans as setting tires free
On Graindor Hill and watching them roll into Route 63
Or breaking into drugstores for only a fistful of shekels
And a couple bottles of Codeine, that false shore
On which he closed his eyes, practicing at shamanism
And stumbling into the literal flumadiddle of *Genesis*,
Research for his thesis in some alternative universe perhaps.

But it's a slow process, an accrual of data
Re-output as material substance, as an object

Not unlike a mandala or an aluminuminous can
From which all of us might or might not drink
As we salute the map that got us here to Storybook Hill
Overlooking Blue Lake and the sleeping fingertips
Of Zephyr City. O truth, O pardners, roll up the map
And stand it in my pocket, the night is tonedeaf
As the sailor on shoreleave who, no Bohemian
Waxwing, wanes poetic to this poor young woman
Who has told him three times, her name is Distance,
She lives just over the border, in Brideshead,
And yes, she works for Sexcalibur, but not tonight
So he should go elsewhere to seek such knowledge
Her heart-shaped box could confirm, that indeed he exists
Not unlike a stake, to be driven into the ground.

The cord of wood around which an event of some significance
May occur, or else, the old man will simply piss.
This is farm country, where Jethro can see more
With one hand than I can see with two eyes. "Oh, say,
Have you been to the Lilies of the Fishes? You just have
To see it, especially now [in the fall]." A pinecone
"Woah," flies by, "Hey, who threw that?" It pushes the myth
Of Renaissance gold, that each rough-hewn idea
Having trekked through North Woods must seat itself
In the mudroom and remove its boots if it intends
To develop a true course of action or tend to
The rosebushes round the burgeoning edge of a green poet's mind.

He sits like a hare behind the wheel of his Stanza, straps
On his seatbelt, turns his key in the ignition. The car starts
It's rendition of "Rock of Ages". Nothing imaginative
Happens this time. It doesn't have to be that way

With poems. It could be anybody's objects in mirror
Are closer than they appear; thus, the insistence
Of desire, not unlike the way we continue to film
In black and white long after the invention of color,
As if to capture something else: something
Other than the usual apples, plums, bananas,
Grapes, dark and light, and pears
In the fruit bowl on the small kitchen table
Which is really boxes of books with a blanket thrown over;
Something, not exactly recordable. In shadow though,

The whole arrangement potbellies in one blue swirl,
A withershins blue which exists only for the covers
Of the philosophy readers of the world. Even today,
The first day of spasms in advance of the millennium,
Black and white film is taken up by the heart all tangled
In extension cords, confused by its etymon, it forgets
It docks in the main cove of the body, it forgets
It's core and cords are more like felspar although
They have lent themselves rightfully to rhythm
And blues. In any event, the heart so to speak
Shoots in black and white, as if to achieve an artistic
Integrity not unlike the employment of regular
Meter or at least look-alike stanzas, right, uh-huh.

But then, someone's mother calls him and tells him,
Your brother has a tumor the size of a lemon
Wedged behind the wall of one of his lungs
The surgery is Friday and if you can make it
Home before then, you know, your brother would love
To see you. And just like that, ten-plus years
Of silence between brothers is broken by

The mother's voice, two thousand miles away.
But how can the poet even begin to bridge
The gap between a tumor and his own impatience
At the traffic light?—the arrow
Finally ours—it doesn't get any greener—
Yet the guy in the first car refuses to pay
Attention. Then, there's the sneaking suspicion . . .

If the intersection is a kind of crossroads and a
Crossroads is a kind of bridge, where's the rub?
Does an obliviousness creep up on us as well?
A refusal to be distracted, to lose focus on the economy
And in a paradox obey the lemon light? Meanwhile
On the other side of Gotham City, Batman's stuck
In traffic, daydreaming of Catwoman, fiddling
With the radio. "Let's talk about gemstones—"
If I knew which one I wanted, I wouldn't have to look
At so many. It's true. Although I picture her with something dark
Like a black diamond, perhaps she might like that
Before I deliver her to the commissioner. Now,
Where's I-75 and why didn't I take it?—Oh, one moment
You're in heaven and the next you're left wondering
What route you could have taken not to be where you are.

Why sum parts, like leaves, parts, in two, in four,
In six, and up, up and away, in the same way that it's hard
To marvel at the marvelous things that happened before
One was born without like meditating on them—
A man has walked on the moon ho-hum, TV appears
And brings us live subordinations from existences
Elsewhere, a plane piloted across the Atlantic, a man
Rises off the earth and penetrates a cloud . . . science

Is promiscuous and one has to wonder what might be different
If we have not come down from the thousands of years
Of mere patriarchy. What jaboticaba frambesia
Might bear, endure? As it is now, I woulda hada be scareda
Myself, the way I am steeped in my own critical
Disputes, taking on my own private apocalypse
Every time I get caught in the passerby's unwitting glance—
Am I not the one I would normally endear myself to?

A pile of dishes, a stack of papers, a molehill of bills,
And books on the table, books on the desk, books
On the fridge, books on the toilet, books on the speakers,
Books on the floor and books on the books on the floor
Like the books on books on the boxes of books
Under the table, in the closet, in the middle of the floor—
We need an apartment just for our books, though not
So much as some people need an apartment.
Pointed as a steeple, there's that certain slant or cramp
Of light which can't be denied, or can be
But shouldn't if you want one hundred percent
True love like who washes the steeple of dishes in the sink?

Not the president of the United States, I can tell you that
And this too: you can throw away your IQ
And your GREs, your ten thousand dollar collection
Of CDs, Your Mary Kay cosmetics, your 183 pounds
Of muscle, and your debt to infomercials and the eighties,
We get the heebie-jeebies and try to shrug it
Or walk it off like a cramp, when that doesn't work
We make a pact to eat more healthfully, we head down
To Marshall's and then to Stop-and-Shop—
We bought a bowl for fruit and now we're going

To fill it long-term. On our way home we stop and sign
Up for kung fu. The kicking will be good for us, will really
Get our aggressions out and exacerbate our sexlife.

With a heart-shaped metal frame containing a metal tongue
We'll make beautiful not-this—not-that music together
And if we appear as monsterbots from outerspace
To the other pedestrians in the park, we won't care but caravan
Until no less than the stars fall for you and I and our song
Tracing the mysterious, lazy-ass and hard-working S
Of the universe oh see—I just used the F word again
Damn it, all things familiar fall: pencils, flowers, books,
Apples and grand pianos, people, planes, even birds,
And those all unfamiliar things, they only rise to fall too
To that dominant Y marks the spot, but it's why
I suppose we come together, that and because there is even an
X like you out there, why we tangle in each other
Like interlocking C notes and say, "To hell with class."

Relentlessly obscure, it really stands out, the way things happen
In autobiography. I mean, shoals of consistency
Are shouldered throughout, by definition, of course, like
As meaningless a phrase as "organized religion," let's
Cut through the cheese, I have a chase to get to, a liberating
Bond, not unlike the one between poet and reader and
Don't give me no shit about I'm supposed to be
Some kind of co-creator and your piece the place
Where the distinctions between poet and reader dissolve
I mean I'm willing to hammer away, but I just spent
Eleven hours on the clock and another two hours
In commuter traffic only to return to a sink full of dishes
That's another half-hour to scrub the essential pot and

Utensils and cook me up some Prince spaghetti, so
I did my job now show me you've done yours.

Seems fair to question the motivations and to what extent
They might be absolved by a graceful finish,
But he's never iceskated, never wanted to, and doesn't
Plan to, so he tells her. He actually did skate once
When he was three, maybe four, with his mother and father
Before they divorced. It was cold, the ice cracked
And so they went home. Testicles are mundane
This really happens! His mind is like this, a hillside
Up which a boulder of thought begins to ascend
Not to roll back down again, but to just suddenly halfway up
Disappear, in its place another often smaller boulder,
Like a midnight snack at three AM where cold cereal's
Desired but you end up with a peanut butter–sardine sandwich.

She was a master of shadowgraphs but didn't know a measure
From a gutter, so I told her if she was serious about
Self-publishing this book she wrote on the general pleasures
And therapeutic applications of shadowgraphy, then
She ought to let me help her with the design and composition,
Which made me feel good about myself because I found
That I really cared about this project of hers as much as
I wanted to fuck her and chalked up my proposal
To "courting" in the Age of the Personal Computer,
But what I didn't know was that she wanted
To fuck me too, this made our relationship easy
At first, but auld cliché, we offered each other nothing
But sex and work, so before you could say, *omigod, omigosh*,
We were through to the realm of thoughts, prayers, and
   remembered and wished-for speech.

Then and next, the matter of recurrence. Where and when
Not to. Does it even make sense? You can stand
To one side, twirling your hair or tugging your beard
In the thrall of page one, as if at a lineup to point
Out the villain, but the information wasn't there, see
You don't have to point, or the information
Was there, the villain wasn't, isn't, won't ever be
There, and there isn't a point to be made beyond
The points that accrue, nothing less innocent
Than a bear-skin rug, while offscreen something like TNT
Rattles the form, proves the foundation, pours a concrete
Confetti over the fields and streams, streets and malls
To put you in debt as soon as can can, a grave debt I,
Your customer service representative, mispronounced death.

Confronted with skepticisms, linguistic, empirical,
And otherwise shambling all around, the only
Invective: Wing it. Like a bird with at best a guess,
A person, poet, desperate as prayer when there's no question
To answer on the mountain's otherside, just some trees
A cloud, and us standing on somebody else's horizon, determined
And fractured as we may be, with my hands, my ears
My eyes my tongue my feet, my yes small heart
Of whatever these amount to, whatever form
That assumes, like the creeping *one, two, three, now
Stand* of standing, all of that admitted wanting
Before the emergency of suddenly knowing a thing
Might not bring what it brings, like sex
Like cancer, a sizeable wallop,
A funky uppercut of wind from the westward shoulder of
   the interstate sky.

IV

ROUTE

after Tristan Tzara

What is this path in the woods that separates
us as I reach across it roses
bloom in place of fingertips while
the other side of the path is pushed
so deep into the distance it is
the rose that circles you as you
walk—less and less knowingly—away

MYSTERY AND MELANCHOLY OF A STREET

for KC

The abandoned U-haul
Hunched over, weight
On its one missing wheel,
Empty except for a three-
Legged oak chair
And a 25¢ coupon
For Zout stain remover,
Squat on the brown lawn
In front of a blue vinyl
Seven-family Victorian,

In shadow, in approaching
Shadow, at the corner of
Summer Street and Vine.
Slowly audible, the laughing
Of a young girl, rolling
Her hula-hoop down, waves
Into the air. No, that's no
House sparrow or starling
Flying overhead, it's a passenger
Pigeon from God knows when.

In the first-floor window,
Opened halfway, a candle
Stands, sending up smoke
Unaffected by the breeze
Which blows only in the distance,

Flapping the flags at Liberty
Park, way off to the west,
From which direction approaches
The shadow of a man, or something
Like a man, pike in one hand, recorder in the other.

THE SECRET OF FLIGHT, A TRIPTYCH

THE FLING

A kiss in
a parking lot
then
kneeling
in the dirt.

THE SHEDDING

I start rearranging myself. I know no one can see the roofs. The trees play with you just like I can. The sun is on my side, because I see beyond this room and the things I have to have. I have discovered twisting. When I stretch, my eyes stay put to save morning. I stretch all the way to Europe. Is Europe not worth saving? Instead of away, where will I be this fall? So I wrap around you. I back in, deciding I may want you for myself again. Like a snake more or less *(but just where and how?)* upon returning each coil chooses to touch you. There. Maybe we need another body to turn it the way it does like meditating light upon your body, cells & head. To the next room, where stretched out, I keep twisting toward morning, you and me on the tanned hide of a drum, instead of away.

THE BELL

This morning
21 times
you plunked
my waist.

VAULT

after Tristan Tzara

the skyscrapers slant against the diagonal sunset
cars turn down one-way alleys never to be heard from again
the pigeons obstruct the scenic views of the park
where the most hospitable properties hide behind the branches
and the squirrels like leaves somersault to the dirt

you walk but there's another who walks in your footsteps
taking his own temperature every five minutes
and reciting the times tables to twelve
wearing a flannel robe that reeks of smoke and mouthwash
earmuffs deaf to the curdling sirens streaming by

the city nauseous with catcalls and flashing lights
its many eyes like saucepans boiling over
spills its tears into the sewers and subterranean abodes
dreaming of the meat of the sterile plains and the way
a kind of white lava polishes the mercurial thermometer sky

finally lost like a keepsake in the history of an obscure rose
your face in my mind and my mind in this city
I roam the narrow streets that surround you
while you yourself roam other more impressive streets
that must surround something

ACCESS

after Tristan Tzara

welcome the magic gait of nights not yet complete
nights drunk in haste like cheap American booze
nights buried under the welcome-mats of our backward passions
sterile dreams fit for the lingering looks of insatiable crows

soiled soaked-through shreds of night still we raise
in ourselves each one of us an idyllic tower so towering
that the view is no longer obscured by mountains or rain
the sky no longer turns away from our trawls for stars
the clouds lie down at our feet like hounds
and we can look the sun in its eyes until oblivion arrives

and yet my free time finds sense and satisfaction
only in the nest of your arms the tide of the night
after the bursting of thunderstorms into currents of mourning
is the body abstracted from its earthen armor
which extracts now the gold from the necklace of our dreams of
    oblivion

POP MUSIC EPISTEMOLOGY AND THE PROSPECT OF VIRTUAL BEING

for John Briggs

Michael Jackson's "I'm Starting with the Man
in the Mirror" is blaring from the clouds.
We've been living in the Motel Foucault forever
now, half-awake and half-dreaming, half-
and-half being poured into our coffee mug hearts.
The signs in the café windows spur us on
to revolution: Put a pair of Nikes on your feet!
It is a country of apples—killed for the pie—
where a few dozen fly balls that fly over the fence
will get you everything you ever wanted and
leave you wanting more, or where you can wash
your clothes for just a dollar and then dry them
for a dollar—if they get dry the first time around.
At the end of Batterson Drive in New Britain, Con-
necticut, one of America's many cul-de-sacs,
a family is riding their new bicycles in circles;
that sound they're making, is that what the music biz
calls white noise? Yes, I believe in the community
of wraiths living in the Seattle area who spend
their days writing on presidents of all denominations.
I have one of their one dollar bills on the wall
over my desk: it has a sketch of the Golden Arches
angled and towering over a crowd of workers
with arms outheld, hands open, in the top right corner
scribbled in red ink it says "Grand-cul." One two
dollar bill I saw once read: "The value of nothing
is worth more than the price of everything in

every mall that's ever existed put together, etc."
But wait, there's a serious debate on TV tonight:
"Why keep publishing books when they don't
even come with laugh tracks: How elitist!"
But first a few poetic words and surreal images
from their sponsors—Hypnosis rises like a
horse from a sleep of tubes and wiring, hoping
to return with a rider, or better yet, a wagon.
Oh god, is it Christmas already? The vampire
kids are not singing the blues, but the praises
of dying on a day like today. Hands in
pockets. War-paint dry on their flour-faces.

SUBTERRANEAN APARTMENT BLUES

Another sunny Thursday
   but no light falls on
The Penguin Rhyming Dictionary
   left open to -**oo**

among floppy disks and envelopes
   on the desk below
the stick-propped, bush-blocked
   half-a-window.

AN ORIGIN

things. The sun starts in the middle of
a phrase its starlight pilgrims
wholeheartedly through the dust and grime
from one end of the black forest
to the other less audible and blacker
end. Why let anything blur
to step over a wave and into a fragment
in the middle of a single breath all
the brave hands of a perfect future past
sealed under a cement surface
and left helpless as any old sequence
of events where the clocks turn just fine
as sand in the eyes of the eternal
pilgrims slackens and burns not eternal
anymore. The movements of a sleeping man
in which a machine comes to life
to understand pain in the sound of rain-
water plopping from gutter to porch
and ends up hammering away
at the white-haired skull of its creator
before the movements of a woken woman
in the movie-blue light of earth at night
as satyr-shadows blow their horns
and flies bemoan the milky rash of dawn.

ALL RIGHT, THEN, I'LL GO TO HELL

with Kristin Citrone

Five after something. The Zoot Sims record is over
and now there's just the sound of me typing
in this half-light, where words are written in blue
and bodies are colored in with purple magic marker.
Tangy nursery school smell I never left behind
and the kid next door listening to Nirvana.
Outside, the hospital's alive, breathing in bodies,
expelling ambulance drivers, growing ivy on the skin
of its tallest brick walls. And all I want to do
is eat. The chicken's out, but I can't douse this
it-has-to-be-writ lit compulsion, this circling complaint
from a posse of mosquitoes. Blood already
withdrawn, the test results pending. Tomorrow
—fuck, I don't know. The past is still
ahead of us, that's the way I see it, that's the
reason I keep on keeping dawn in a drawer
in the nightstand beside my single hospital bed.
I lie on sheets stained with spaghetti sauce, my hands
lost in smoke—but who do I know that smokes?
The cat next door? The newsman saddling his blonde
palmetto, divorcing his old thunderbird? I suffer
no deadlines, just my own self-flagellation and will
to break the heart of the world, as if words
themselves could wheel a carriage
through every eventual outcome, crying
"Which way to the Advanced Poetry Workshop?
Which way to self-actualization? Which way
to mass self-destruction?" The main instruction's to avoid

sounding like rock lyrics. The beat goes on
like a battery commercial, and I'm chanting along:
"Vanitas. Thanatos. Recess. Ellipsis,
I guess." The cat's green eye, or the child's
green-black marble, rolling into and out of the circle
of confetti. Nostalgia too. So where am I now?

SOME RESEMBLANCE ACQUIRED

with Kristin Citrone and Nicole Henderson

Collage me. Make me up out of little pieces:
Face of our latest serial killer, coupon for diet soap.
This new romanticism has tentacles made of trash,
two-way eyes, blue Valium skull. And the new millennium?
Homeopathic electronics, antique televisions, just
another Postmodern Reader displayed on the shelf.
I will now collaborate with myself, a solitary twin,
and make art out of postcards. Wish you were here
in this vertigo, the future, cracking my neck
into shards of light. The splash of corporate beer
seeps into a high-heeled blister on the ankle bone
of a purple woman. Everything is odd at a trendy
angle of metaphor. Everything sifts through the purple
woman who is me under this calm, uncertain moonlight.
But I'm no woman, and this is not the age of amethyst;
the sun is a high blue diamond and our only hope
belongs to the scientist: genetic manipulation, micro-
waveable organs, template fashion. Whatever
we think when I walk by in leather skirt and tweed coat,
throwing pizza crusts at the pigeons, denying the sidewalk
cracks which swallow me. Whole.

EPITHALAMIUM

with Kristin Citrone, Nicole Henderson, and Chris Mulia

The small air. My arms behind me. Night
through the window I am not looking out
like some raggedy blue parrot, but I am
waiting for someone to light the candle,
waiting like lint in an empty pocket, waiting
like an empty can on the roadside for some
anybody to come and pick her up, and
the sun is . . . or maybe it isn't, I can't tell
anyone about the pain in my spleen.
Pink tissue paper and a pair of scissors
cure my relaxation. I am not confused
or bitter. An entire lifetime hidden—
thwarted desire and something yielding
uh huh, the wire heart hanging from the ceiling
of our house of cards like a musical ornament
broken in a fit of lamenting that made
the neighbors look out of their windows lovingly
at the three-day old roses I threw in the trash
this morning. Romance ends in a heap of
memoir. Maybe the story's essence
is where I'm not sure. Whoever she was, we are,
she was certainly not dawn, which happens
to be stretching out now, all swan and red.

OUTSTRETCHED STREETLIGHT AQUA SERENADE

with Kristin Citrone

Fresh sweat on a white Kleenex
we take off our clothes
and throw them over the sun

All the pretty blue bonnets pulled
tight over our eyes
the whites of our eyes brush up
against the cloudless sky

Sugar cookies baking in a lemon sauce
our twenty toes touching down
on seven globes at once

Dolphins swimming in my sauce pan
get beached on soggy saltine islands
Outside on earth
another fire engine sears by

THE LOVER

after Paul Éluard

She is arisen from my lids,
Her hair entwined in mine.
She has the shape of my hands,
She has the brown of my eyes.
She's swallowed in my shadow
Like a stone thrown at the sky.

She has her eyes always open
And never lets me sleep.
Her dreams in broad daylight
Make sunshine evaporate,
Make me laugh, sob and laugh,
Talk, though I've nothing to say.

AGAINST THE YEARS OF GREAT MOMENTUM AND LOSS

A song I want to sing that ends in breathsmoke
Leaves me hanging like a cigarette but
In any event I wander seeking to avoid emergencies
Like compromise and couldn't fit a sunburst
Pattern in my mouth to go with those I've loved
And lost because untrampled grass exists
Between the (so-called) natural dimensions of improvisation

I drag myself down by my own blue cuffs
Why of course there is no other way now is there
A way to make sense between doorways
And the lack of doorways in certain problematic poems
It turns a key which in turn starts a car
And if it is not an it than it must be a she is not far
For laughing at the innocence of such filth

As the television whaling against the avatar of nights
Turning away the camouflage of dawny grays
Which combine to form the nucleus of a kind of a leap
Procured by a squirrel thru the piss-ant of time
From one monkey-wrenching log of watery decay
To leaky hallucinations of a blondie in heat
Melting his hands to the dog bark of the horizon

NIRVANA RONDEAU CENTO

I miss the comfort in being sad
And the sound of electric guitars
Dowsed in mud, soaked in bleach
The sun shines in the bedroom
In my face—Spring is here again

And all the flowers have gingivitis
And cock and twist and masturbate
I wanna jump! This isn't right!
I miss the comfort in the sun

In the toilet bowl, aroma cloudy
It's the sulfur in and out of a dream
Of a marigold—Oh take my bed
And leave a blanket of ash on the ground—
The sun is gone—it's what I am—
I miss the comfort—no más

WHAT WHOLE? WHAT SUM? WHAT PARTS?

The ocean sky, the yellow sand,
A lawn chair, a mass market in hand,
Who can smell the hot dog stand
As it happens at the moment

An exuberant, more intimate form
Of democracy is obsolete,
And so "the detail" of the conventional
Demarcations of desire, implicit

In performance, excludes an upheaval
Of the present that is both voluptuous
And political, where absence is
Grace, that manual of detachment

As mystification, as technique
For attenuating the ways in which language
Is the literal participant in the body
That seeks the exemption from meaning,

Not unlike a chair, a book, to find
Some connection, and yet nothing to say:
As air is to fire, to ocean, sky:
Renewed upon contact, emptying away.

PEACEWARD RECOIL

after Baudelaire

Be calm, my despair, play it cool for once.
You called for dusk, now dusk's come down
To bury the city in its dark romance:
What's peace to some, shakes others by the bone.

Now watch how wanton men bare their backs
To pleasure's whips, and beg for chains, condemned;
They treat remorse to a series of circus acts.
Mad despair, lend me your hand, follow my lead

Away from such things—until wasted years splay,
In butterfly collars, against the sky's rails;
And regret emerges on the shore, all smiles;

And the dying sun seeks dreams under a bridge,
While, like a veil trailing in the east for miles,—
Listen, my sweet, hear?—night's soft steps approach.

POEM

for Archie Ammons

A feather
floating upward
for no
apparent reason,

only to
reverse itself
and make apparent
sense.

LATE

Someone else will play
a mountain. You stay
the phone, say, "Hello,
I'm afraid." Our window

will cloud, inside, and
the wind will empty
outward from the city
the blue phonebooths in

bluer rain. No stars
will leave you for
the different future where
Death, miffed, will steer

for another as I
walk away not knowing
a mountain, no stars
when I call you.

PART

for Tom Clark

The door of undress and removal of days
inches out toward night. Goodbye poets!

Lady Madonna! The art of you waits with
muddy bottom, tiny bell, and mattress eyes

cast in berry light. Wisdom narrows
to a blue kiss in which what creaks in darkness

shuts as the orgasm around me—O tambourine!—
parts like mind from trembling water.

ABOUT THE AUTHOR

Scott Keeney is the author of *Early Returns, Pickpocket Poetica,* and *Sappho Does Hay(na)ku*. His works have appeared in *Columbia Poetry Review, Mudlark, New York Quarterly, Poetry East,* and elsewhere. He lives with his family in Connecticut.

www.ingramcontent.com/pod-product-compliance
Lightning Source LLC
Chambersburg PA
CBHW051348040426
42453CB00007B/462